STORIES of the SAHABA

THE MIGHTIEST MUSLIM HEROES

UMM HANEEFA

ILLUSTRATED BY SHAMEEN RATHNAYAKA AND GOLAM MUNIM

Published by Fig and Olive Press

First published 2025

002 - Second Edition

Written by Umm Haneefa

Edited by Mohammad Abdul Mojid

Text and cover copyright © Umm Haneefa, 2025

Cover art designed by © Umm Haneefa, 2025

Illustrators: Shameen Rathnayaka and Golam Munim

Illustrations by © Canva

All rights reserved

The moral right of the author and illustrators has been asserted

Set in Alata std/ 11 pt

Typeset design by Umm Haneefa

Printed and bound in the UK

All rights reserved. No part of this publication may be reproduced or transmitted in any form or by any means, electronic or mechanical, including photocopying, recording, or any information storage or retrieval system, without prior permission in writing from the publishers and/or author/illustrator.

ISBN: 978-1-73-969258-2

STORIES
of the
SAHABA

THE MIGHTIEST MUSLIM HEROES

UMM HANEEFA

ILLUSTRATED BY SHAMEEN RATHNAYAKA AND GOLAM MUNIM

Please note that the illustrations in this book are symbolic. They are not to be taken literally and are not attempts to depict the sahaba themselves.

For the one who earned me this kunyah ♡

A sincere heartfelt thanks to Bukhari Institute's Zakir Ahmad and Sadique Hussain who combed through each and every line for authenticity.

Your support, alongside the help of Yuvanis Foundation, has been invaluable.

Jazakumullahu khairan.

CONTENTS

Map	Page 9
Author's Note	Page 11
Khadijah bint Khuwaylid ﷺ	Page 13
Bilal ibn Rabah ﷺ	Page 19
Sumayyah bint Kayyat ﷺ	Page 25
Suraqa ibn Maalik ﷺ	Page 31
Mus'ab ibn 'Umayr ﷺ	Page 39
Nusayba bint Ka'ab ﷺ	Page 47
Hudhayfah ibn Al-Yaman ﷺ	Page 53
Umm Waraqah ﷺ	Page 61
Khalid ibn Waleed ﷺ	Page 67
Asmaa Bint Abi Bakr ﷺ	Page 73
Bibliography	Page 82
About the Author	Page 83

JERUSALEM
KHAYBAR
MOUNT UHUD
TABUK
MADINAH
BADR
HUDAIBIYAH
MOUNT THAWR
MOUNT NOOR
SAFA
MARWA
MAKKAH
RED SEA
TAIF
HABASHA
N
E
S

In the name of God, the Most Gracious, the Most Merciful

AUTHOR'S NOTE

There'll be days where it seems like the world works against us. There'll be times when it'll feel like our faith is not enough. There'll be moments when holding onto our deen becomes a struggle. When that happens, I want you to spread wide these pages and find a home here. This history of ours is rich - and it's a reminder of who we truly are. We're the bravest of leaders, the most courageous of warriors, the greatest of thinkers and so much more. We are heroes in our own right, bi idhnillah.

Dear reader, have faith.

Do not take lightly that we are of the ummah of Muhammad ﷺ. We bear the banner of Islam like beacons of light. We owe it to ourselves to learn from the past - and so to pave a way for a future that's better.

So when your heart becomes heavy, find yourself here. Keep faith. Remind yourself of the best of those who came before us - and perhaps (if God wills) we'll unite with them in the best of homes in the Hereafter.

Umm Haneefa

'The best people are those of my generation'

Prophet Muhammad ﷺ

Sahih al-Bukhari 6429

KHADIJAH BINT KHUWAYLID ﷺ

THE MOTHER OF BELIEVERS

'I was blessed with loving her.'

Sahih Muslim, Book on the Merits of the Companions, in al-Nawawi, vol. 15, p. 197.

Deep in the bustling markets of the Arabian peninsula was a wealthy business woman by the name of Khadijah bint Khuwaylid ﷺ. Khadijah ﷺ was born into the Banu Asad tribe and was admired for both her beauty and her excellent character. Over time, she lost many of those closest to her. The deaths of her parents, her first husband and then her next, meant that Khadijah ﷺ was the richest woman in the whole of Makkah because of the inheritance left to her and her children. However, it wasn't her money that was her legacy, or her ability to make it so plentifully. Little did Khadijah ﷺ know that she would not only become the first convert to Islam, but she would also have the honour of being the first to comfort the Prophet ﷺ when revelation from the Qur'an first began.

In pre-Islamic Makkah, it was hard to find an honest merchant to trade alongside. It was common knowledge that those who worked in the markets would cheat and lie for personal gain. Many a time, Khadijah ﷺ had hired someone to trade for her, only to have them give her little in return while they pocketed more profit themselves. One day, Khadijah's ﷺ sister Hala told her of a man who had been shepherding her flock. Amongst his people, he was known as As-Saadiq and Al-Ameen (the Honest and the Trustworthy), and his name was Muhammad ﷺ. Keen to hire him, Khadijah ﷺ had to make multiple offers to Muhammad's ﷺ uncle Abu Talib before he finally agreed to let him travel to Syria with her caravan.

The year that Muhammad ﷺ took Khadijah's ﷺ caravan for trade was the year Khadijah ﷺ made the most money in business. Even more so, Muhammad ﷺ gave all the profits to her. Khadijah's ﷺ servant Maysara, who accompanied him to Syria, told her of the miracles surrounding the man she had hired. In the beating heat of the desert sun, the clouds would gather to offer him shade and the trees would bend their branches to do the same. In her heart, Khadijah ﷺ knew that Muhammad ﷺ was a man like no other. After spending years refusing proposals from the most notable men of the Quraish, it was Khadijah ﷺ who sought out Muhammad's ﷺ hand in marriage. At the age of 40, Khadijah ﷺ wed for the final time and began to fall in love with the 25 year old Muhammad ﷺ.

Life with Khadijah ﷺ was filled with affection and comfort. They were even blessed with the gift of children: four daughters and two sons. While the girls flourished and filled their home with light, Khadijah ﷺ and Muhammad's ﷺ boys passed away at a young age. Despite his sadness, Muhammad ﷺ only grew ever closer to Khadijah ﷺ. They were the best of companions and marrying Khadijah ﷺ meant that the poorer way of life that Muhammad ﷺ had grown accustomed to was forgotten for some time. Khadijah ﷺ brought him a new honour and status, and it was one that would only become greater when one day his life changed forever.

It was Ramadan. The skies were dark and the stars had settled into the night sky. Muhammad ﷺ had retreated to the cave of Hira for his usual practice of praying. Suddenly, the angel Jibreel descended and overwhelmed him, commanding him to recite! The small cave was flooded with light and words that Muhammad ﷺ had never before uttered revealed themselves:

"Recite in the name of your Lord who created,
Created man from a clot.
Recite, and your Lord is the most Generous,
Who taught by the pen,
Taught man that which he knew not."

Shaken with fear, Muhammad ﷺ rushed back home and into Khadijah's ؓ arms. For a while, there was only silence between them as Khadijah ؓ held him tightly. When he finally spoke, Muhammad ﷺ confessed his worries and what had happened. He began to have doubts, thinking himself mad. But Khadijah ؓ just held him tighter, reassured him, and reminded him of who he truly was. Muhammad ﷺ was a man of truth and these were glad tidings from his Lord.

That day marked the moment the Qur'an was first revealed, raising Muhammad ﷺ to the highest honour of a Prophet of Allah. Amidst everything, it was Khadijah ؓ he chose to run to and it was Khadijah ؓ who gave him hope. Despite their lives changing tremendously that day, and despite the long hardships they would face afterwards, Khadijah ؓ remained (until the very end) Muhammad's ﷺ most beloved companion. She was the first to accept Islam and the first to hold the honorary title of Umm al-Mu'mineen, the Mother of Believers. She had faith in Muhammad ﷺ when he had lost it in himself and she, for her sacrifices and her love, was promised her place in Paradise.

DID YOU KNOW?

After the conquest of Makkah, when Muhammad ﷺ came back to the land he had fled from all those years ago, he was asked by the people where he would make his home. Muhammad ﷺ was offered the most luxurious of them all, but he turned each and every one down. In the end, he pitched his tent in Al-Hajun, next to the grave of Khadijah ﷁ.

BILAL IBN RABAH ﷺ

UNBROKEN AND FREE

'O Bilal, tell me of the most hopeful deed you practised in Islam. I heard the scuffle of your sandals before me in Paradise.'

Sahih al-Bukhari 1149, Sahih Muslim 2458

In the early seventh century in the old lands of Makkah, there lived a young man by the name of Bilal ibn Rabah ﷺ. Even though he was born and raised in the Arabian deserts, Bilal's ﷺ family had long ago been stolen from their homeland in Habasha (modern day Ethiopia). His mother had been sold into slavery when she was just a child and it wasn't long before Bilal ﷺ wore the very same chains.

Soon afterwards, a new religion called Islam was spreading in the heart of Makkah. Because many of the nobles had hated what they heard about it, people whispered about these new teachings of equality and community in hushed voices. It seemed that those who welcomed Islam into their homes and their hearts would face a difficult fate.

One day, while serving his master (a nobleman of Makkah), Bilal ﷺ overheard the gathering men. They were worried and scared that their way of life was being threatened. Thus they continued to mutter amongst themselves in anger and spite. How could a mere tradesman by the name of Muhammad ﷺ be preaching freedom and fairness? How could a 'lowly' slave be equal to his owner? How could a poor man stand side by side with a king? The noblemen couldn't afford to let this happen. They agreed that Muhammad ﷺ must be stopped, whatever the cost.

In the corner of the room, unnoticed by anyone, Bilal ﷺ became excited. Unless his ears had deceived him, there seemed to be a way for his people to be free again. For too long, black people had served in chains. Bilal ﷺ needed to know if he could help put a stop to that.

It was then that Bilal ﷺ began his journey to Islam, but being black meant that it certainly wasn't easy. When his slave-master finally found out about Bilal's ﷺ faith, he tied him up and tortured him under the heat of the desert sun. Yet still Bilal ﷺ refused to let go of his religion and the nobles only made things worse for him.

"Ahad, ahad," Bilal ﷺ gasped as more rocks were pressed against his chest. He pointed a finger skyward, struggling to catch a breath. "One, one!"

Despite the torture, Bilal ﷺ continued to call Allah and Muhammad ﷺ grew increasingly worried. There was no way that Bilal ﷺ would survive this punishment. In desperation, Muhammad ﷺ turned away from his friend, searching for someone to free him. It was then that Abu Bakr ﷺ paid the price for Bilal's ﷺ life.

The slave-master laughed in his face. "Had you but given me one coin," he said. "I would have sold this useless slave."

Abu Bakr ﷺ stood firm in his stance, determined to defend his friend. "Had you asked me for 100 coins, I would have given this for Bilal."

From that day on, Bilal ﷺ was treated more like an equal by his closest friends and he became one of the dearest companions of Muhammad ﷺ too. He was even given the blessing of calling the adhaan, the Islamic call to prayer (an honour nobody else was given at the time). Years later, at the conquest of Makkah, when Islam spread across the land it began in, it was Bilal ﷺ who entered the city gates in the presence of other noblemen. It was Bilal ﷺ who ascended the Ka'bah to make the call to prayer.

DID YOU KNOW?

Bilal ibn Rabah ﷺ was one of the few companions who was actually promised Paradise. One day, the Prophet Muhammad ﷺ approached him and told him that he had heard Bilal's ﷺ footsteps before him in Jannah.

SUMAYYAH BINT KHAYYAT ﷺ

THE FIRST MARTYR

'Receive glad tidings, O family of Yaasir, for you have an appointment in Paradise.'

Mu'jam Al-Awsat 1535

Over 1400 years ago in the old lands of the Arabian kingdom, there lived a fierce woman by the name of Sumayyah ﷺ. Like many of those who were enslaved at the time, she was originally from Habasha, but had lived her life in Makkah. Despite facing such hardships, Sumayyah ﷺ had a spirit that could not be broken. Little did she know that this spirit of hers would allow her to leave a legacy that the Muslim world would never forget.

Sumayyah ﷺ and her husband, Yaasir ﷺ, along with their son, Ammar ﷺ, served one of the most powerful tribes of the Quraish at the time – the tribe of Banu Makhzum. Banu Makhzum was widely known for its wealth and leadership, and they certainly did not want anybody to compete against their power. So, in time, when Muhammad ﷺ started spreading the message of Islam, telling people that power belongs only to Allah, the people of Banu Makhzum saw him as a threat. One of the nobles in particular, Abu Jahl, was determined to see his end by punishing anybody who followed him.

When Sumayyah ﷺ finally learned about Islam, she eagerly accepted it. At the time, because of the threat made against the believers, many of those who embraced Islam kept it a secret for fear of persecution. Sumayyah ﷺ, however, was one of the first of seven people to boldly make it known that she, in fact, was a follower of the faith. But being a black woman enslaved to the tribe of Banu Makhzum (a tribe who now saw her as an enemy as opposed to their own) meant that her life was about to become harder than it had ever been before.

When word had spread that the family of Yaasir ﷺ had converted to Islam, Abu Jahl was furious. He refused to accept that a family serving his very tribe had dared to disobey him. Blinded by anger and fuelled by rage, Abu Jahl swore he would get revenge.

Sumayyah's ﷺ family had no protection of their own. Unlike Muhammad ﷺ, they weren't natives of Makkah and nor had they any allies to support them. As such, they became Abu Jahl's very first victims. One day, when the heat of Makkah reached its highest point, Abu Jahl dragged Sumayyah ﷺ, Yaasir ﷺ and Ammar ﷺ into the streets and forced coats of iron upon them. Under the scorching desert sun, the metal burned like fire, blistering and branding their skin. When Abu Jahl asked them to curse the Prophet ﷺ or renounce the religion of Islam, they raised their heads and refused.

Hell-bent on proving the family of Yaasir ﷺ wrong, Abu Jahl took their torture further. He tried every punishment he could think of, each becoming more violent than the last – yet it was Sumayyah ﷺ who didn't yield. Instead she glared into Abu Jahl's eyes and praised Allah the Almighty, and His messenger ﷺ.

Worse still for Abu Jahl, Sumayyah ﷺ had drawn a crowd who all saw her defiance and bravery. Instead of humiliating the family of Yaasir ﷺ, Abu Jahl's plan had backfired. The nobleman thought he could break them easily into submission, simply because they were poor and because they were black. Clearly, he had underestimated their conviction, meaning he was the fool instead. It was even said that the Prophet ﷺ had comforted Sumayyah ﷺ, saying her family's place was in Paradise. It seemed that these words alone were comforting for her.

One day, Abu Jahl decided enough was enough. He tied Sumayyah ﷺ to the trunk of a tree, giving her one last chance. In front of a crowd, he taunted her viciously, but Sumayyah ؓ stood her ground.

"I swear," she said to Abu Jahl, despite all the pain that had been inflicted upon her. "You are smaller in my sight than a beetle on the ground." Then she raised her voice louder and invoked the name of Allah.

With this, Abu Jahl couldn't stand his humiliation any longer. He grabbed a spear and took her life. Upon her death, Sumayyah ؓ saw a glimpse of the paradise she was promised – a blessed gift granted to so few in this life. Sumayyah ؓ, in that moment, became the first martyr in Islam. To this day, she stands as a heroic symbol of courage in the face of injustice and oppression.

DID YOU KNOW?

Sumayyah's son Ammar ﺭﺿﻲ ﺍﻟﻠﻪ ﻋﻨﻪ, after seeing his mother and father die, renounced his religion. After he was released, he ran to the Prophet ﷺ distraught, explaining how it was the torture that made him say it; in his heart, he truly didn't believe what he had said to Abu Jahl. It was then that Allah revealed verses of the Qur'an in response to him, clarifying that there was no blame upon Ammar.

SURAQA IBN MAALIK ﷺ

THE BOUNTY HUNTER

'In the first part of the day Suraqa was an enemy of Allah's Prophet and in the last part of it, he was a protector.'

Sahih al-Bukhari 3911

There came a time in the old Makkan lands when the Prophet's ﷺ life was in imminent danger. News had reached the Quraish that the oasis of Yathrib was being prepared for the Messenger's ﷺ arrival. If Muhammad ﷺ made it there safely, Islam would spread and flourish. This would pose a threat to the idol-worshipping way of life that the Quraish had loved so dearly. Because of this, the tribal chieftains had decided that enough was enough! After over a decade of tolerating Islam, it was time for them to end it once and for all.

One evening, the leaders of the Quraish tribe gathered together. In hushed voices, they called for the assassination of Muhammad ﷺ, As-Saadiq Al-Ameen (the Honest and the Trustworthy). He was to die at their hands that very night.

The year was 622 CE and night had fallen. Outside of the Prophet's ﷺ house, a crowd of angry men had gathered. Bloodthirsty and bearing masks to hide themselves, they clutched onto spears and swords that glinted in the moonlight. All they had to do was wait.

Suddenly, just before daybreak, the armed men burst into the Prophet's ﷺ room. They raised their swords to strike… only to find Ali ibn Talib ؓ, Muhammad's ﷺ cousin, in his place. Furious, the tribesmen stormed the rest of the house. They had been tricked! The Prophet ﷺ had escaped from their very clutches!

There was no time to waste. If the Prophet ﷺ reached Yathrib, it would be too late. In desperation, the men upturned every home Muhammad ﷺ could have taken refuge in. Yet still there was no sign of him.

It was then that Abu Jahl, the enemy of Islam, declared a bounty on the Prophet's ﷺ head. Anyone who returned Muhammad ﷺ to him, dead or alive, would be rewarded with 100 camels!

All at once, the streets of Makkah buzzed with life. It was all anyone and everyone could talk about. Abu Jahl watched this frenzy and smiled. For him, it was only a matter of time.

Meanwhile, a little way away, news of a wanted man reached Suraqa ibn Maalik ؓ. Suraqa ؓ wasn't a city-dweller nor had he paid attention to the rise of Islam. He was a skilled horseman whose knowledge of the desert was second to none. If anyone had known the tracks of the wild like the back of his hand, it was Suraqa ibn Maalik ؓ. The bedouin hunter had devoted his life to the likes of this.

Swiftly on horseback, Suraqa ؓ raced to Abu Jahl.

"Three nights," he said to the chief. "Give me just three nights and he's yours."

Abu Jahl nodded as Suraqa ؓ, like many before him, prepared for the quest.

It wasn't long before Suraqa ﷺ found the traces of Muhammad's ﷺ footsteps, as well as those of his companions. The hunter followed the tracks carefully until he saw the shadows of travelling men in the distance. His eagle eyes scanned the horizon. It was them. He was sure of it.

Suraqa ﷺ whipped his horse, determined to cross the desert quickly. The Prophet ﷺ and his companions were close. Just a stretch further, he thought. Just a stretch!

All of a sudden, Suraqa's ﷺ horse jolted. The bedouin was flung skyward before landing in the sand with a thud. With the thought of 100 camels still on his mind, Suraqa ﷺ reined his horse in and tried again. Just as he began to close the gap between them, Suraqa's ﷺ steed sank its hooves into the sand, throwing him more violently than before. The bounty hunter couldn't hide his confusion. Never in his life had he experienced this before. He was a man who had travelled far and wide. He was skilled in the art of war. He could even count the number of troops making their way to battle simply by seeing their tracks. But at that moment, Suraqa ibn Maalik ﷺ was baffled. Whatever power was protecting Muhammad ﷺ, it was working.

Despite this, desperate for his reward, Suraqa ﷺ ignored the signs and tried again – only to fail once, twice and three times more. It was only when he was close enough did he call out to the Prophet ﷺ himself.

"Enough!" Suraqa ﷺ shouted, raising his hands. "I will do no harm. Let me speak with you."

Gradually, it was like an invisible shield had been lifted for the hunter could finally approach the Prophet ﷺ and his companions. With his sword by his side and his arrows behind him, Suraqa ﷺ greeted Muhammad ﷺ, Abu Bakr ﷺ and Amir ibn Fuhayra ﷺ.

"This business of yours, this religion," Suraqa ﷺ began, glaring at the men intently. "I know it will spread far and wide."

The travellers remained silent.

"When you come to my tribesmen or wherever I may be, I want your word that I will come to no harm. I want your oath to say that I will be safe." Suraqa ﷺ waited. Before him was a man who had the price of 100 camels on his head, a man who so many of the Makkans wanted dead. Yet here he was, walking under the beating sun of the desert at peace. Whatever Muhammad's ﷺ cause, Suraqa ﷺ was convinced it would succeed. He was a rider who had set out to make the Prophet ﷺ his prisoner; in return, Suraqa ibn Maalik ﷺ had begged for his protection instead.

The Messenger ﷺ granted the horseman his request and had it scribed on a parchment. Just as Suraqa turned to leave, Muhammad laughed gently.

"How will you be, O Suraqa, when you are wearing the bracelets of Kisra?" he asked.

Suraqa was astonished and taken aback. "Kisra! Kisra? The son of Hormuz?" Kisra so happened to be the most powerful king in the world at the time, the head of the formidable Persian empire. Kisra's bracelets were known around the world to be one of his most precious possessions. How could they possibly make their way to the bedouins of Arabia?

The Prophet simply smiled and turned away.

Suraqa never forgot what was said in the desert that day. The words of the Prophet stayed with him, even after Muhammad's death. It stayed with him too after the death of Abu Bakr, the khalifah who succeeded him. For Suraqa, what happened would stay with him until the very end.

Years later in Makkah, during the governance of Umar ibn Khattab, Suraqa watched a caravan arrive from the kingdom of Persia. The expedition had been successful and, in just one year, the Muslims had defeated one of the most powerful empires of the time. The king had fallen and his palace was stripped of its most valuable possessions.

"O Suraqa," Umar ibn Kattab called, handing him treasures from the spoils of war. "Hold up your hands."

Suraqa did as he was told. It was then that Umar placed in them the bracelets of Kisra. It was then that the promise of Prophet Muhammad came true. The treasures of Persia's most powerful king had made their way to the bedouins of Arabia.

DID YOU KNOW?

Suraqa ibn Maalik ﷺ held onto the little parchment containing the Prophet's ﷺ oath. During the conquest of Makkah, almost a decade later, he returned to the Messenger ﷺ and presented it. It was then that the huntsman declared his acceptance of Islam.

MUS'AB IBN 'UMAYR ﷺ

THE GOOD

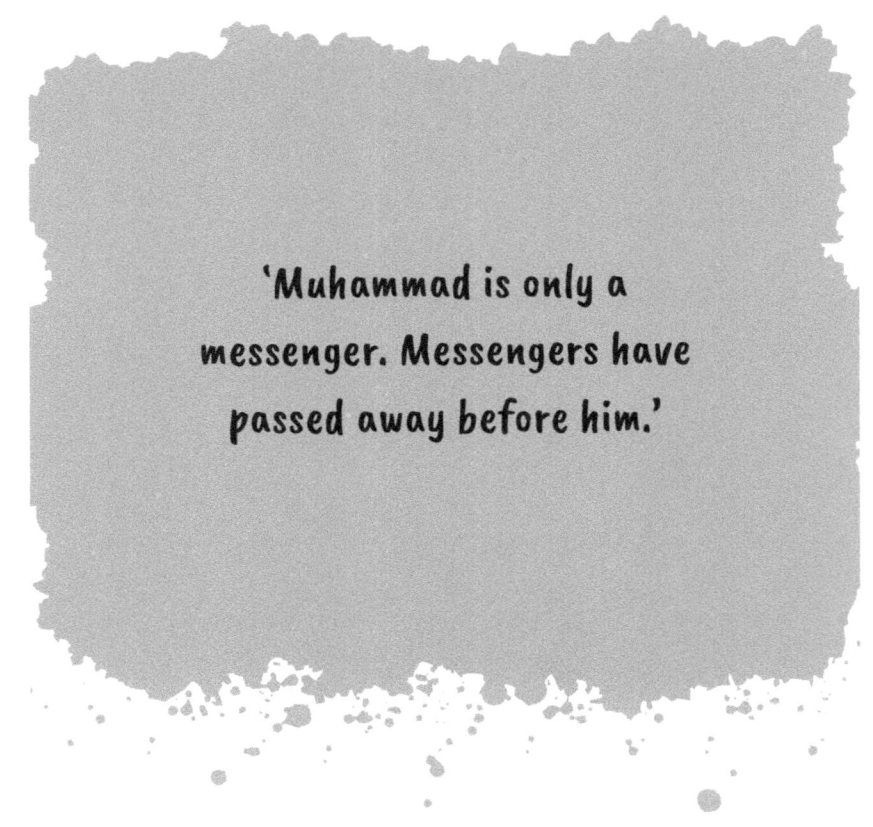

'Muhammad is only a messenger. Messengers have passed away before him.'

Surah Al-Imran: Verse 144

A long time ago in the early Makkan lands, there lived a young man by the name of Mus'ab ibn 'Umayr ﷺ. Mus'ab ﷺ happened to be the son of wealthy parents, both of whom (his mother especially) doted on him lovingly. Under their roof, Mus'ab ﷺ was given all the things he ever wanted. Even the noblemen of Quraish warmed to him. Being wise beyond his years meant that he was allowed to attend the meetings of the most powerful tribes of his time. It seemed that his way with words and his elegant style had truly endeared the hearts of the Makkans.

Over time, the oasis of Makkah was bustling with talk of a new religion. The voices in the markets and whispers in the streets grew louder. Muhammad ﷺ, a man widely known for his sincerity and trustworthiness, was preaching Islam – a faith that threatened to destroy the Quraish way of life.

Undeterred by the anger of his allies in Quraish, Mus'ab ﷺ made his way to the House of Al-Arqam where rumour had it that the believers were gathering. It was there that he met the Prophet ﷺ and his followers, who were few in number at the time. Mus'ab ﷺ listened to the words of the Qur'an intently. When Muhammad ﷺ welcomed him, placing his hand upon Mus'ab's ﷺ chest, a feeling of peace overwhelmed him. It was then that Mus'ab ibn 'Umayr ﷺ embraced Islam, offering his skills and service to his newfound faith.

Despite his conviction to Islam, Mus'ab ؓ had one major problem to overcome: the anger of his mother. Khun-nas bint Maalik was a formidable woman who very few dared to cross. The noblemen of Quraish could wage a war of words against him and it would matter very little. However, one slight from the mother who had raised and cherished him instilled fear in his heart. As such, Mus'ab ؓ decided to hide his faith, believing this was best.

But in every corner of Makkah, there was always someone watching. There was always a whisperer spilling secrets to Quraish. It wasn't long before Mus'ab's ؓ mother and the rest of the tribes heard about the betrayal of his conversion. Livid, Mus'ab's ؓ mother tied him with chains and imprisoned him in the very home he grew up in. Mus'ab ؓ remained there under the watchful gaze of his mother's guards.

One day, Mus'ab ؓ heard that a group of Muslims were making their way West to Habasha where a just king reigned the land. There the Muslims would find safety and security. Desperate to flee, Mus'ab ؓ waited for the perfect moment to escape and join the others. That day, Mus'ab ؓ not only fled from those who kept him prisoner, but he also sacrificed the life of luxury he had been so accustomed to.

Times were difficult for the Muslims then. They faced harshness and hardship almost everywhere. They had no state of their own and no real place to call home - even if the likes of kings protected them. Setback after setback made the hearts of the Muslims heavy. News also had it that the Prophet's ﷺ latest call to Islam in Taif ended in bitterness. It was shortly afterwards that Mus'ab ﷺ was given one of the most important responsibilities for a follower at the time; he was to be sent to the oasis of Yathrib to use his charisma to preach the religion of Islam. If he was successful, the Muslims would finally have a home of their own: a place to practise their religion freely without the fear of persecution. Muhammad ﷺ himself had given Mus'ab ﷺ the task over those both older and seemingly wiser than him. Mus'ab ﷺ was determined not to let him down.

As fate would have it, Mus'ab's ﷺ expedition to Yathrib was a successful one. By the way of his grace (and no doubt the help of Allah), the tribes of Yathrib quickly turned to Islam. People converted to the religion in masses - the young and the old, the meek and the strong, and even the most powerful of tribes. Soon Yathrib was buzzing, preparing for the arrival of the Prophet ﷺ. Mus'ab ﷺ became the first envoy of Islam and his success meant that Yathrib became the first place to embrace Islam, a city later renamed Madinah.

Mus'ab ﷺ lived a life full of service to Islam and even his end was a noble one. Back then, battles were still brewing against the Muslims, and the time came when the call to war was made. After their losses in Badr, the Quraish were determined to get revenge. Consequently, for the Battle of Uhud, the Prophet ﷺ called upon Mus'ab ﷺ to carry the Muslim standard, the flag bearing the banner of Islam. In the midst of all the chaos, after the Muslim army thought they had won, the Quraish led a surprise attack against them. They had finally caught the Muslim fighters off guard. The Muslim ranks had now been infiltrated. The Prophet ﷺ himself was vulnerable. Many had believed him dead. Seeing the Quraish gain the upper-hand, Mus'ab ﷺ had to do something.

Mus'ab al-Khayr ﷺ raised the standard high. With a sword in one hand and the flag in the other, he flung himself into the fray.

"Muhammad is only a Messenger," he bellowed. "Messengers have passed away before him!"

Suddenly, a horseman from Quraish plunged at him, severing his right hand in retaliation.

"Muhammad is only a Messenger," he repeated, raising the standard with his left hand with all his might. "Messengers have passed away before him!"

Another strike from the Quraish caused his left hand to be sliced off too. Still Mus'ab ﷺ didn't waver. He held up the standard with all that was left of his bleeding arms, crying "Muhammad is only a Messenger! Messengers have passed away before him!"

It was then that a spear from the enemy took his life. It was then Mus'ab ibn 'Umayr ﷺ was martyred. As he fell, the standard he died defending fell with him.

After the battle, when the hearts of the Muslims were heavier, the Prophet ﷺ grieved openly. He had lost his beloved uncle Hamza ؓ (the Lion of Allah), he had lost his close companions, and he had lost Mus'ab ibn 'Umayr ؓ. The Prophet ﷺ wept over his body. Mus'ab ؓ, who had once worn the finest of attires, now lay with a burial shroud that wasn't enough to cover him. Here lay the youth who once had all of life's luxuries, and he who had ultimately given it up in the way of Allah. The loss of Mus'ab ibn 'Umayr ؓ was a devastating blow to the Ummah, but his service was one that would never be forgotten.

DID YOU KNOW?

The graves of the martyrs slain during the Battle of Uhud, including both Mus'ab ibn 'Umayr ﷺ and Hamza ﷺ, can be visited in Saudi Arabia to this day. Many hajj and umrah tour guides include the visit to the Shuhada Uhud Cemetery during the pilgrimage there.

NUSAYBA BINT KA'AB ﷺ

THE SHIELD OF THE MESSENGER ﷺ

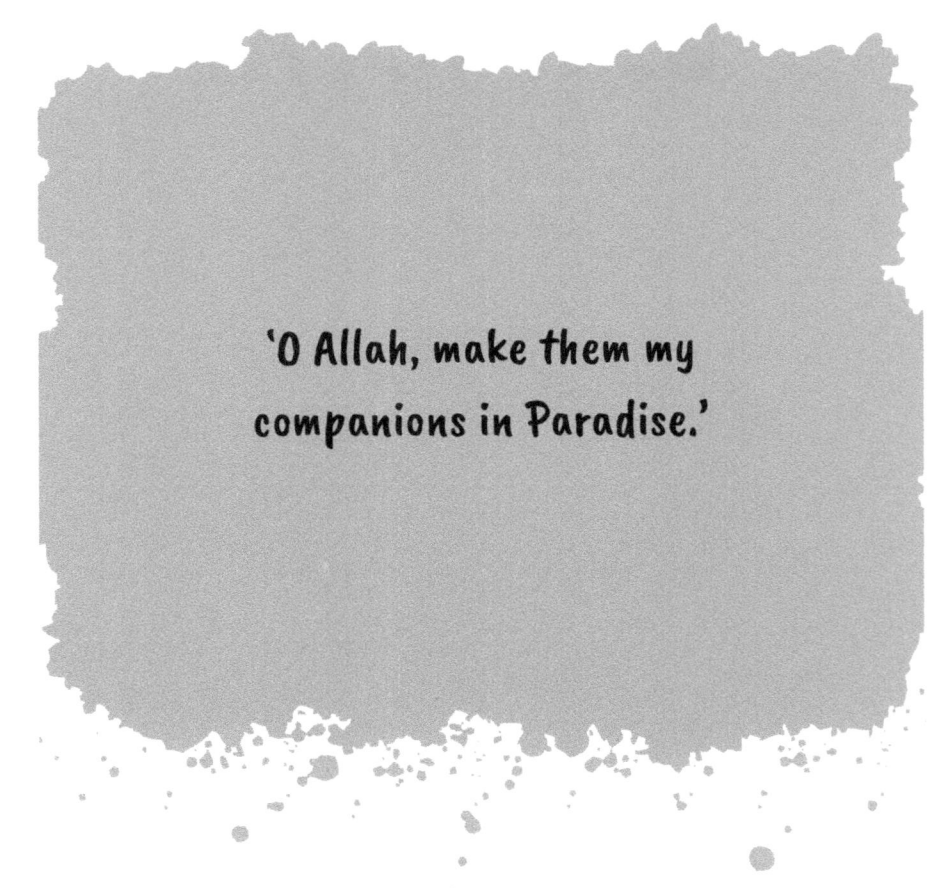

'O Allah, make them my companions in Paradise.'

Ibn Sa'd in al-Tabaqaat al-Kubra (8/415)

Over a thousand years ago, in the desert lands of Arabia, there lived a fierce young fighter by the name of Nusayba bint Ka'ab ﷺ. Nusayba ﷺ was born to the Banu Khazraj tribe in Madinah and she was skilled with a shield and sword. But back then, even Nusayba ﷺ couldn't have known that she would be remembered across the Muslim world as one of the most courageous warriors of her time.

One day, news travelled to the bustling oasis of Nusayba's ﷺ home. The Prophet Muhammad ﷺ was making his way to Madinah. He was coming with the message of Islam and Nusayba ﷺ was among the first to accept the new religion. In fact, Nusayba ﷺ was one of only two women given the honour to pledge their allegiance in the valley known as Al-Aqabah. It was from that day on that Nusayba ﷺ swore to protect the Prophet ﷺ at all costs. It was from that day on that she became one of the Ansaar, the Helpers of Muhammad ﷺ.

However, in time, it became clear that not everyone was happy with the new way of life that Islam brought with it. Very quickly, battles began brewing in the deserts of Arabia and soon the call to war was made. Nusayba ﷺ gathered her weapons and stormed forth on horseback. She was determined to keep her promise of protecting the Prophet ﷺ. She would not let him down – not while she was alive.

True to her word, during the Battle of Uhud, Nusayba ﷻ swung and slashed her sword fiercely. She knew that the enemy was getting closer by the second. Her friends, her family and her foes clashed with each other, attacking to protect their own.

In the middle of the battle, in the corner of her eye, Nusayba ﷻ saw the Prophet ﷺ struggle and fall. Immediately, she carved her way towards him. The Prophet ﷺ swung around to see his saviour and realised it was none other than Nusayba Bint Ka'ab ﷻ. With a sword in one hand and a shield in another, Nusayba ﷻ plunged her weapon into her opponent's horse, sending its rider skywards. She, with her family, continued to defend the Prophet ﷺ as the spears ripped through the skies and war cries filled the horizon.

When the battle had ended, even though the Muslim army had lost, the Prophet ﷺ approached Nusayba ﷻ as she cleaned her wounds. It was then that he made a du'a just for her and her family alone. The Prophet ﷺ prayed that he'd be with them in Paradise for all their courage and their bravery.

Nusayba bint Ka'ab ﷻ fought alongside the Prophet ﷺ in the many battles that came afterwards. It was her skill as a warrior and her faith in Islam that made sure her legacy of bravery lived on long after she had left this life.

DID YOU KNOW?

One day, Nusayba bint Ka'ab ﷺ asked the Prophet ﷺ why the Qur'an seems to address men instead of women. In answer to her, Allah revealed verses, telling her that men and women were equal in the eyes of Islam.

HUDHAYFAH IBN AL-YAMAN ﷺ

THE KEEPER OF SECRETS

'The hypocrites of today are worse than those of the lifetime of the Prophet ﷺ, because in those days they used to do evil deeds secretly, but today they do such deeds openly.'

Sahih al-Bukhari 7113

Back in the 7th Century, in the old lands of Arabia, there lived a young boy named Hudhayfah ibn al-Yaman ﷺ. Hudhayfah ﷺ was born in Makkah, but grew up in the oasis of Yathrib (now Madinah). His family was one of the first there to accept the new teachings of Islam.

Growing up, Hudhayfah's ﷺ parents, al-Yaman ﷺ and his mother ﷺ, were devoted to their faith. They taught him all about the kindness and wisdom of Prophet Muhammad ﷺ and his belief in one God. In awe of their stories, Hudhayfah ﷺ longed to meet him one day. With age, his desire to meet the Prophet ﷺ only deepened. The young man followed every inkling of news about him, hoping their paths would cross. Finally, the day came when Hudhayfah ﷺ decided to travel to Makkah to meet the Prophet Muhammad ﷺ himself.

Upon meeting the Prophet ﷺ, Hudhayfah ﷺ asked him a question that had preoccupied him.

"Am I a Muhajir (one who has migrated from Makkah) or an Ansaari (one who has helped the Prophet in Madinah), O Messenger of Allah?"

The Prophet ﷺ smiled kindly and, to his surprise, gave him the choice.

Hudhayfah ﷺ thought for a moment and decided to be amongst the Ansaar, believing that this was where his heart truly lay.

After the Prophet ﷺ and the Muslims migrated to Madinah, Hudhayfah ؓ became very close to the Messenger ﷺ. He joined him in almost all the important battles, including the Battle of Uhud, where he fought bravely alongside his father, al-Yaman. However, the pressure of the battle was intense. While Hudhayfah ؓ emerged safe and sound, sadly, his father met a different fate. Al-Yaman ؓ had been left with the non-combatants because he was old, but he decided to join the battle anyway. In the chaos of the fighting, some of the believers mistakenly attacked al-Yaman ؓ, not recognizing him. Despite Hudhayfah's ؓ desperate cries for his father, the old man fell and was slain.

While mourning, Hudhayfah ؓ showed incredible forgiveness and restraint to those responsible for his father's death. When the Prophet ﷺ offered to compensate Hudhayfah ؓ for his loss (a common practice at the time), Hudhayfah ؓ refused, saying his father had attained the honour of martyrdom - something he had long desired.

Hudhayfah's ؓ wisdom, bravery, and ability to keep secrets continued to impress the Prophet Muhammad ﷺ. This was so much so that he trusted Hudhayfah ؓ with a very important task: to keep secret the names of the hypocrites amongst them (those who pretended to be Muslims, but secretly plotted against them). This was a heavy responsibility, but Hudhayfah ؓ accepted it with dedication. Because of this, Hudhayfah ؓ was given the honorary title 'The Keeper of the Secret of the Messenger of Allah.' In doing this, he protected the believers by keeping a close watch on the hypocrites, ensuring they couldn't harm the Muslims from within.

Being so trusted by the Prophet ﷺ meant that Hudhayfah ؓ was given responsibilities very few could dream of. As such, there came a day when he was given a dangerous mission, one that put his life on the line.

The year was 626 C.E. The Battle of the Trench had stretched over weeks and the Muslims were surrounded by enemies at every turn. Ahead of them was the Quraish led by Abu Sufyan, a man who wanted the Prophet ﷺ dead. Behind them was Banu Qurayzah, a tribe who betrayed the believers and sided with their foes. Worse still, the harsh conditions of the desert had weakened the Muslims. There was nowhere left to turn. In desperate need of a new strategy, the Prophet ﷺ sent Hudhayfah ؓ to sneak into the Quraish's camp at night to gather their military intelligence. Under the cover of darkness, against a fierce wind that raged against him, Hudhayfah ؓ infiltrated the ranks of his foes. Treading carefully, Hudhayfah ؓ blended in so that no one would notice him.

Suddenly, Abu Sufyan gathered his men to speak to them.

"O people of Quraish," he began, "I have something important to say, but I'm afraid it might reach Muhammad. O people, check who is sitting next to you."

Hudhayfah ؓ knew he had to act quickly. If he was exposed, he wouldn't leave the camp alive. He swiftly grabbed the hand of the man next to him.

"Who are you?" Hudhayfah ﷺ asked sharply. The man was startled and hastily answered, clearing Hudhayfah ﷺ of any suspicion.

Abu Sufyan continued, "We are not safe here. Our horses and camels are dying, Banu Qurayzah has abandoned us, and this cold is too difficult to bear. Our fires won't stay lit and our tents are useless. It's time we leave."

Abu Sufyan gathered himself and mounted his steed. Hudhayfah ﷺ knew that this was his cue to flee too. Armed with the knowledge that the enemy were beginning to retreat, the decision was made for the Muslims to hold their ground a little longer. Victory would soon be theirs.

Hudhayfah ؓ continued to serve Islam in the many battles that followed, even after the death of Muhammad ﷺ. He played a key role during the expansion of Islam into Iraq. After distinguishing himself in several battles, he was appointed governor of important cities like Kufa and Ctesiphon. But no matter his successes in worldly affairs, Hudhayfah ؓ remained humble and modest, fearing his Lord first and foremost.

There even came a day when the people of Ctesiphon were eagerly waiting to greet their new governor. In the distance, they saw a thin man riding a donkey and eating a loaf of bread with salt. To their surprise, the rider was Hudhayfah ؓ - the self-same governor. Despite being given riches of the world as reward for his achievements, Hudhayfah ؓ lived a life of service to his Lord.

DID YOU KNOW?

When Umar ibn Khattab ﷺ became khalifah, he'd ask Hudhayfah ﷺ to testify whether a person was a hypocrite or not. However, Hudhayfah ﷺ (as The Keeper of the Secret of the Messenger of Allah ﷺ) never disclosed any names. True to his character, he kept his word until the very end.

UMM WARAQAH ﷺ

THE PROMISED MARTYR

'Apostle of Allah, allow me to accompany you in battle.'

Sunan Abu Dawood 591

In the beautiful oasis of 7th Century Madinah, there lived a noblewoman by the name of Umm Waraqah ؓ. Born into the Al-Khazraj tribe, her family was known for both their honour and their wealth. However, these weren't the qualities that the Muslim world remembered her for. What made Umm Waraqah ؓ truly special was her love for Islam and her devotion to the Qur'an.

When the religion of Islam spread beyond the borders of Makkah and made its way to Madinah, Umm Waraqah ؓ was one of the early converts who accepted the faith before the Prophet ﷺ even arrived there. The more she learned about Islam, the more she fell in love with it. Very quickly, she began practising her faith. She spent long days reciting, memorising, and following the teachings of the Qur'an. Everything she did, whether in her home or out in the community, was guided by the Holy Book. So it wasn't long before she became known widely for her knowledge and her dedication.

However, a new religion in the heart of Arabia (where the old idol-worshipping ways were still rife) was bound to stir trouble. In time, battles brewed on the horizon and another call to war was made. The Prophet Muhammad ﷺ rallied more Muslims to join his forces in Badr. Umm Waraqah ؓ was amongst the women who responded to his call. She desperately wanted to help nurse the sick in hopes that she would be granted martyrdom - the honour of sacrificing her life in service to the Deen. To her surprise however, Umm Waraqah ؓ was turned away. Instead the Prophet ﷺ told her to return home. He had told her that it would be there that she would find the fate she had so longingly wished for. And so it was from that day on, her people lovingly called her Ash-Shahidah, The Martyr.

Soon afterwards, the victory of Badr was celebrated and time passed for Umm Waraqah ﷺ. She continued to devote her life to Islam. Despite being wealthy and well-respected in her community, she refused to let both the luxuries of life and her status preoccupy her. She had even promised her two servants (whom she treated like children of her own) their freedom after her death. Such was a testament to her generosity and detachment from worldly things. Having no husband and children also meant that Umm Waraqah ﷺ could devote more time to that which she loved most; thus she became a seeker of knowledge and a proficient reciter of Qur'an. This was so much so that the women of Madinah would flock to her home, a place that became known to have the low hum of Qur'an inside it long into the late hours of the night.

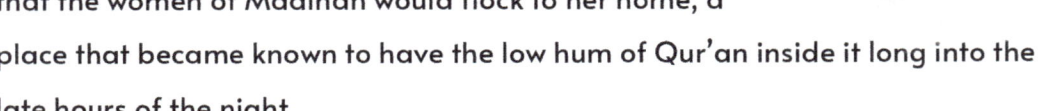

Years continued to pass and it seemed that death evaded Umm Waraqah ﷺ. However, it sadly didn't evade everyone. The year was 632 C.E. and Prophet Muhammad's ﷺ passing brought grief to the ummah. The Muslims had lost the companionship of their Messenger ﷺ, and a new khalifah by the name of Abu Bakr ﷺ was chosen to lead after him. But he too had passed while Umm Waraqah ﷺ lived, and Umar ibn Khattab ﷺ took up the mantle after him.

In time, there came a night when Umar ﷺ conducted his usual night patrols. He noticed that it was quiet. Too quiet. Something wasn't right. When Umar ﷺ passed by the home of Umm Waraqah ﷺ, now in her old age, he noticed a silence he had never heard there before.

When morning came, Umar's ﷺ thoughts remained troubled.

"I didn't hear the recitation of my aunt last night," he said, referring affectionately to Umm Waraqah ﷺ.

As such, the khalifah rushed to her home to put his mind at ease. When he finally reached her, to his sadness, he found Umm Waraqah ﷺ lifeless on the floor. Her house had been ransacked by her servants, who had been tempted too much by the freedoms she had promised them. After they had murdered her, they had made their escape. As Muhammad ﷺ had promised decades beforehand, Umm Waraqah Ash-Shahidah ﷺ was granted her heart's deepest desire of martyrdom. It so happened that the oasis of Madinah had lost a noblewoman who honoured her faith above all else. Meanwhile, the gardens of Paradise had gained the self-same noblewoman who had never faltered in her faith.

DID YOU KNOW?

Umar ibn Khattab ﷺ, the Leader of the Believers, took it upon himself to capture Umm Waraqah's ﷺ murderers personally. They were found quickly and sentenced to death for their crimes.

KHALID IBN WALEED ﷺ

THE SWORD OF ALLAH

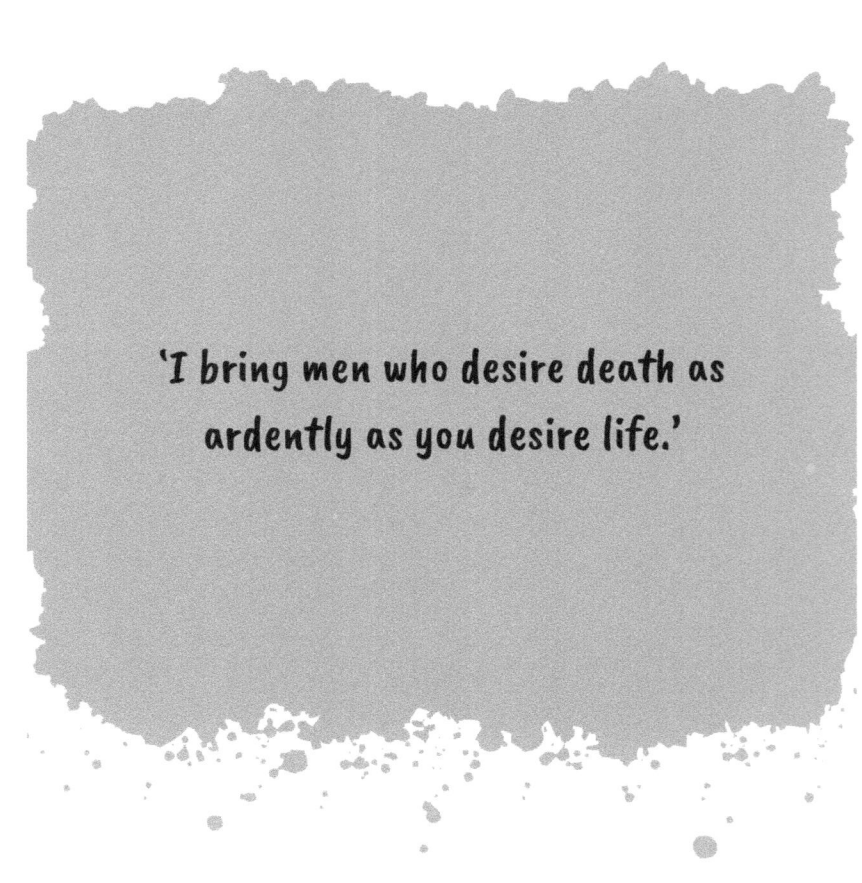

'I bring men who desire death as ardently as you desire life.'

History of the World, Volume IV (Book XII. The Mohammedan Ascendency)

Long, long ago in the early seventh century, there lived a brave, young man by the name of Khalid ibn Waleed ﷺ. Born into wealth and privilege, Khalid ﷺ was raised with riches and power. His father was the leader of Banu Makzhum, one of the most prosperous clans of Makkah's famous Quraish tribe. Yet it wasn't Khalid's ﷺ father who would make him one of the greatest military commanders of the Muslim world; Khalid ﷺ, with Allah's help, would one day make that name for himself.

Growing up, Khalid ﷺ was a skilled swordsman so it was no surprise that he became a warrior in his own might. In just a few short years, taking after his father, Khalid ﷺ became a leading military force in the Quraish.

At the time, a new religion was spreading quietly in the oasis of Makkah and, unsurprisingly, not everyone was happy with this new way of life. The noblemen of Quraish couldn't believe that a poor man by the name of Muhammad ﷺ was given prophethood over them. In their eyes, it wasn't fitting for a lowly orphan to compete against a wealthy chieftain. Khalid ﷺ, in particular, refused to become a follower of Islam because he believed that Muhammad was trying to compete in leadership against his father. There was no way that Khalid ﷺ could allow that. In fact, when the time came and battles started brewing across the peninsula, Khalid ﷺ himself went on horseback into the fray, and fought tirelessly against Muhammad's ﷺ soldiers.

One frightful day, during the Battle of Uhud, some of the archers in the Muslim army disobeyed the Prophet's ﷺ command, celebrating what seemed like an early victory instead. When they should have stood firm in the mountains, they fled, leaving their stations and their army unprotected. It was then that Khalid ؓ seized his chance and ordered the Quraish forward. The Muslims were in shock! The tide had turned fiercely. A battle the Muslims thought they had won was going quickly awry. Worse still, rumours had run rife that the Prophet ﷺ had been slain.

That day Khalid ؓ returned to Makkah victorious. Even though the news was false and the Prophet ﷺ had survived, the Muslims (for now) had been defeated thanks to Khalid's ؓ quick thinking and skilled tactics. However, Khalid ؓ wasn't done yet. As long as Muhammad ﷺ was alive, he was still a threat.

One day, the Quraish sent Khalid ؓ along with 200 armed men to attack the Muslims while they were praying salah. Khalid ؓ knew that Muhammad ﷺ would be amongst them somewhere and that this would be his chance to end the religion once and for all. Hiding behind them and out of sight, Khalid ؓ waited for the perfect moment to strike - the moment when the Muslims would be most vulnerable - the moment they bowed low in prayer.

But something caught Khalid ؓ by surprise. When the Prophet ﷺ proclaimed 'Allahu Akbar', only half the congregation fell into sujood, something he had never seen before. When the Prophet ﷺ called out again, the other half kneeled in prostration while the original stood guard. It was then that Khalid ibn Waleed ؓ, mastermind of the military arts, realised that Muhammad ﷺ was protected by none other than Allah. Islam would win the hearts of his people and this Prophet ﷺ before him would lead them whether Khalid ؓ liked it or not. It was then that Khalid ibn Waleed ؓ began his first steps in his journey towards Islam.

One quiet evening when Makkah seemed still, Khalid ؓ put aside the letter his brother had written to him. Waleed ؓ, who was older than him, had accepted Islam years ago and had left for Madinah (a city new Muslims found refuge in). Khalid ؓ hadn't seen his brother since then - yet here his words meant more to him than they had ever done before. Waleed's ؓ letter begged Khalid ؓ to join him and, after gathering his belongings with a trusted friend, Khalid ؓ made his way to Madinah to make his choice.

"As-salamu 'alayka, ya rasool-ullah," Khalid ؓ said, greeting the Prophet Muhammad ﷺ in Madinah as his brother stood beside him.

After declaring his newfound faith, Khalid ؓ became a formidable force for the Muslim ummah. He won battle after battle, expanding to new borders and territories, while spreading the message of Islam. His victories and successes helped earn him the title of 'Saif-ullah', the Sword of Allah. Even after the death of Muhammad ﷺ, Khalid ؓ continued his expeditions to distant lands and remained undefeated until the very end.

DID YOU KNOW?

On his deathbed, Khalid ibn Waleed ﷺ told his companions that, as a warrior, he had wounds on every part of his body – yet he was never bestowed the honour of dying on the battlefield. His companions simply said that when the Prophet ﷺ gave him the title of Saif-ullah, he should have known that the Sword of Allah does not die on the battlefield, and that Allah's sword could never be broken.

ASMAA BINT ABI BAKR ﷺ

FEARING NONE BUT ALLAH

'I have not seen anyone more generous than Aisha and Asmaa, though their generosity was different. Aisha would gather things and after they had been collected, she would share them. As for Asmaa, she would not leave anything for tomorrow.'

al-Adab al-Mufrad 280

Long long ago, in the 7th century oasis of Makkah, there lived a young girl by the name of Asmaa ﷦. She was the daughter of the kind and generous nobleman Abu Bakr ﷦. Asmaa ﷦ was only a child when she heard about the teachings of a new religion being preached by the Prophet Muhammad ﷺ. After learning about the faith of Islam, along with her father, she became amongst the first to convert.

As Asmaa ﷦ grew up, she became known for her courage and strength. She married a warrior named Zubair ﷦, and soon after their marriage, the newlyweds were expecting their first child. Around this time, Makkah had become a dangerous place for the believers. The home they had called their own for a lifetime had become almost unbearable to live in. New Muslims were being captured, tortured and killed by tribal leaders at every turn. This was so much so that Prophet Muhammad ﷺ and Abu Bakr ﷦ decided to flee Makkah and seek refuge in Madinah.

Even though Asmaa ﷦ was expecting a baby, she bravely helped her father and the Prophet ﷺ escape Makkah. She would secretly carry food to them while they hid from those who wanted to harm them. To do this, she tore her waist belt into two pieces, using them to tie up the food. Because of this, Prophet Muhammad ﷺ gave her a special title: 'The Possessor of Two Belts.' He told her that she would be rewarded with two belts in Paradise, promising her place there in the afterlife.

Asmaa's ﷢ bravery didn't stop there. There quickly came a day when an enemy by the name of Abu Jahl, known for his cruelty and tyranny, came to her door. He was enraged because he couldn't find the Prophet ﷺ or Abu Bakr ﷢, and he believed that Asmaa ﷢ knew where they were hiding. Even though Asmaa ﷢ was heavily pregnant and alone, she stood firm in her faith and refused to tell Abu Jahl anything. This made him so angry that he slapped her with great force - yet Asmaa ﷢ refused to give in.

Shortly afterwards, Asmaa ﷢ travelled to Madinah where she gave birth to her son, Abdullah ﷢. Life was not easy for her or her family there either. She and her husband were very poor. They didn't have much, but Asmaa ﷢ worked hard, taking care of their horse, preparing food, and doing all manner of chores. Despite all the challenges thrown her way, she remained strong and faithful.

Years passed and Asmaa ﷢ showed her courage again during the Battle of Yarmouk. It was there where she picked up a sword and fought alongside the other Muslim warriors. The formidable Byzantine enemy (a powerful empire at the time) fell at the hands of the believers. The Muslims emerged victorious and quickly conquered Syria and the Levant.

As Asmaa ﷢ grew older, she began to witness division in the very same ummah that was once united under the banner of Islam. Her son Abdullah ﷢ took the mantle of khalifah across the western Muslim lands. However, his rule came with struggles that would eventually cost him his life.

There came a time when Asmaa ؓ, now 100 years old, welcomed her son into her home for the last time. The air was thick and her heart was heavy. A bloodthirsty governor by the name of Al-Hajjaj had laid siege to Makkah and had attacked the House of Allah. He had slain many of the sahaba already and had convinced a faction of the believers that Abdullah ؓ was not fit to reign the Muslim world. The tyrant, calling himself a true Muslim commander, was given orders to assassinate Asmaa's ؓ son once and for all.

Abdullah's ؓ voice was low with fear that day. "What do I do?" he asked.

Both mother and son were in the privacy of Asmaa's ؓ home, away from those who chanted for Abdullah's ؓ death.

"Do I give up? Do I surrender?" he continued. "Or do I keep fighting?"

Asmaa ؓ looked at him and beckoned him closer.

"By God," she said, holding his gaze. "A dignified strike with a sword is more beloved than a humiliating lash of a whip. Keep your dignity, my son."

Abdullah's ﷺ mother reminded him of the hardships they had faced beforehand. They had survived the early days of Islam. They could bear this too. The family of Zubair ﷺ were warriors. They didn't kneel before anyone beside their Lord.

"But my mother, won't you grieve?" he asked sadly, bowing his head low.

"My dear son, I would grieve if you were killed in falsehood." Asmaa ﷺ whispered. "Alhamdullilah. All praise to the One who made you in a way that Allah loves and in a way that I love. Come close to me, my son, so I can feel you and I can smell you for the last time."

Asmaa ﷺ embraced her son, holding him tightly. He kissed her head as tears fell heavily between them.

"What are you wearing?" she asked him, touching the metal that encased the contours of his skin.

"My armour," murmured Abdullah ﷺ. "I am protected."

Asmaa raised her head and shook it slowly. "This, my son, is not the dress of a martyr."

"But I'm afraid they will kill me," Abdullah ﷺ confessed. "They will mutilate my corpse and they will hang me."

Asmaa ؓ held him closer. "O my son, the sheep is not harmed by the skinning after slaughter. Seek the help of Allah. Seek the help of Allah."

Abdullah ؓ nodded before walking away, preparing himself for death. Before he left, he had one request.

"Do not stop making du'a for me, my mother," he said earnestly, before leaving her one last time.

Asmaa ؓ raised her hands in prayer and fulfilled his final wish.

That day was the day that Abdullah ibn Zubair ؓ was martyred. Al-Hajjaj, in bloodlust, crucified him by the Ka'bah.

Upon hearing of her son's death, even in her old age, Asmaa ؓ charged before Al-Hajjaj defiantly. The tyrant demanded Asmaa ؓ seek his permission to have her son's body returned to her.

"He's a hypocrite," Al-Hajjaj spat with contempt.

Unnerved, Asmaa ؓ branded him a liar.

"Your son has violated the House of Allah, this sanctuary of Allah," he retaliated. "He deserved to be killed. It is Allah who can make him taste the punishment that's owed to him."

Asmaa ؓ, at 100 years old, stood taller and spoke clearly.

"O enemy of God, O enemy of the Muslims, the man you killed was one of fasting. He was one who was in prayer. He was a guardian of the Deen and a protector of his religion. If you have ruined this worldly life of his, then surely he has ruined your hereafter."

Asmaa bint Abi Bakr ؓ stood firm in defence of her son in the face of one of the cruellest leaders of her time. The young woman who had once protected the Prophet ﷺ from enemies in her youth had not faltered in her courage despite her age. She was a woman who held tightly to her faith despite the hardships she had faced. Such was Asmaa ؓ - may Allah be ever-pleased with her.

DID YOU KNOW?

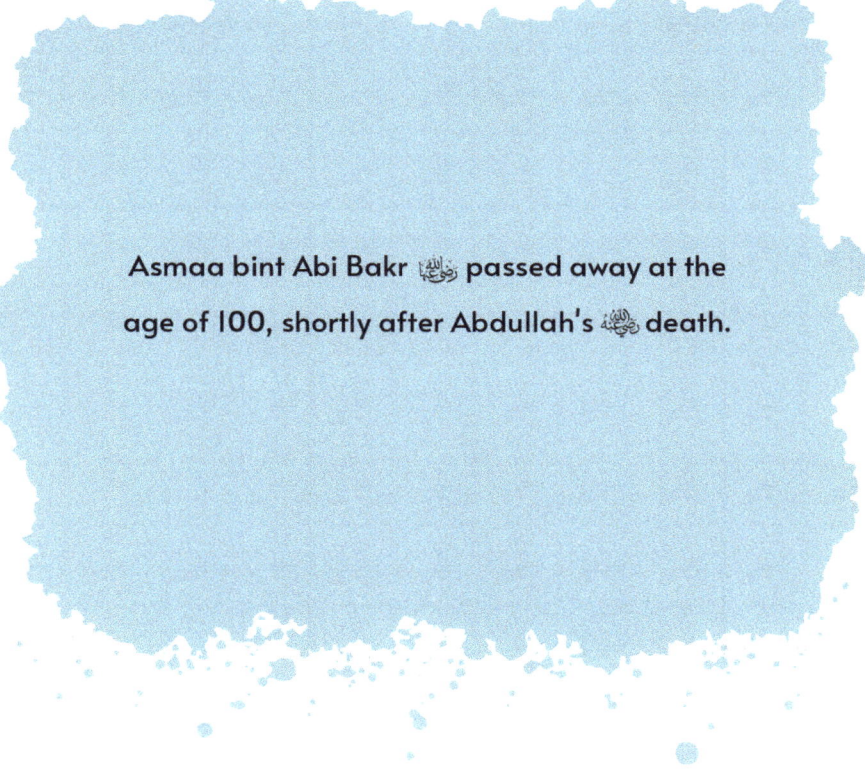

Asmaa bint Abi Bakr ﷺ passed away at the age of 100, shortly after Abdullah's ﷺ death.

BIBLIOGRAPHY

A special thanks to Yaqeen Istitute's Sheikh Omar Suleiman for his THE FIRSTS series

Yaqeen Institute for Islamic Research. (n.d.). Khadijah (ra): His First Love, Our First Mother. [online] Available at: https://yaqeeninstitute.org/watch/series/khadijah-his-first-love-our-first-mother.

Yaqeen Institute for Islamic Research. (2024). Bilal ibn Rabah (ra): The Voice of Certainty | Yaqeen Institute for Islamic Research. [online] Available at: https://yaqeeninstitute.org/watch/series/bilal-ibn-rabah-the-voice-of-certainty-the-firsts.

Yaqeen Institute for Islamic Research. (2024). Sumayyah (ra): The First Martyr | Yaqeen Institute for Islamic Research. [online] Available at: https://yaqeeninstitute.org/watch/series/sumayyah-the-first-martyr.

Yaqeen Institute for Islamic Research. (2024). Suraqa ibn Malik (ra): The Bounty Hunter | The Firsts | Yaqeen Institute for Islamic Research. [online] Available at: https://yaqeeninstitute.org/watch/series/suraqa-ibn-malik-ra-the-bounty-hunter-the-firsts.

Yaqeen Institute for Islamic Research. (2024). Musab Ibn Umair (ra): The Man Who Gave It All | The Firsts | Yaqeen Institute for Islamic Research. [online] Available at: https://yaqeeninstitute.org/watch/series/musab-ibn-umair-ra-the-man-who-gave-it-all-the-firsts.

Yaqeen Institute for Islamic Research. (n.d.). Nusaybah bint Ka'ab (ra): The Woman Warrior | The Firsts. [online] Available at: https://yaqeeninstitute.org/watch/series/nusaybah-bint-kaab-ra-the-woman-warrior-the-firsts.

Yaqeen Institute for Islamic Research. (2024). Hudhayfah ibn al-Yaman (ra): The Secret Keeper | The Firsts | Yaqeen Institute for Islamic Research. [online] Available at: https://yaqeeninstitute.org/watch/series/hudhayfah-ibn-al-yaman-ra-the-secret-keeper-the-firsts.

Yaqeen Institute for Islamic Research. (2024). Umm Waraqa bint Abdullah (ra): The Martyred Hafidha | The Firsts | Yaqeen Institute for Islamic Research. [online] Available at: https://yaqeeninstitute.org/watch/series/umm-waraqa-bint-abdullah-ra-the-martyred-hafidha-the-firsts.

Yaqeen Institute for Islamic Research. (n.d.). Khalid ibn al-Walid (ra): Becoming the Sword of Allah | The Firsts. [online] Available at: https://yaqeeninstitute.org/watch/series/khalid-ibn-al-walid-ra-becoming-the-sword-of-allah-the-firsts.

Yaqeen Institute for Islamic Research. (n.d.). Khalid ibn al-Walid (ra): The Legendary Military General | The Firsts. [online] Available at: https://yaqeeninstitute.org/watch/series/khalid-ibn-al-walid-ra-the-legendary-military-general-the-firsts.

Yaqeen Institute for Islamic Research. (n.d.). Asma Bint Abi Bakr (ra) : The Possessor of Two Waist Belts. [online] Available at: https://yaqeeninstitute.org/watch/series/asma-bint-abi-bakr-the-possessor-of-two-waist-belts.

ABOUT THE AUTHOR

Umm Haneefa is a secondary school teacher and storyteller who is passionate about empowering the next generation of the Muslim youth. She taught English Literature in several schools across the north of England before stepping away from mainstream education. After a brief stint in leadership in private education and home-schooling, Umm Haneefa launched Fig and Olive Press, a Muslim indie publisher that is determined to serve her community. STORIES OF THE SAHABA is the debut title from the press.

Lately, Umm Haneefa has been spending the majority of her time spinning stories with her little one and eating her weight's worth of toddler leftovers. Her ambition is to weave stories that convey the beauty of Islam for the children who come after her.

If you enjoyed reading this book, please consider leaving a review and sharing it with others. Word-of-mouth within the community means a lot to indie authors.

www.ingramcontent.com/pod-product-compliance
Lightning Source LLC
LaVergne TN
LVHW072017060526
838200LV00060B/4695